NATIONAL
GEOGRAPHIC

T0080633

Ladders

Exploring
Above and
Beyond

Read to find out how rocket scientist Robert Goddard paved the way for human space flight.

Reaching
for the
MOON

by Rebecca L. Johnson

Robert Goddard was a rocket scientist and engineer. His dream was to travel to the moon. Today he is considered the father of modern rocketry, or rocket science.

The moon is Earth's closest neighbor in space. Throughout history, people have dreamed of traveling there. The invention of telescopes in the 1600s allowed people to look closely at the moon and see the details of the surface. Yet when people first calculated the moon's true distance from Earth—384,400 kilometers (238,855 miles)—traveling there seemed impossible. The distance is like traveling around the Equator nine-and-a-half times!

American scientist and inventor Robert H. Goddard believed it was possible to get from Earth to the moon by using a rocket. As a teenager, Goddard loved reading science fiction stories. He was particularly impressed by H.G. Wells's book *War of the Worlds*, in which creatures from Mars invade Earth.

When Goddard was 17, he began to think seriously about space travel. "I imagined how wonderful it would be," he wrote, "to make some device which had even the possibility of ascending to Mars." From that point onward, Goddard devoted his life to making space flight a reality.

In 1920, when he was 37, the Smithsonian Institution published a scientific report by Goddard titled "A Method of Reaching Extreme Altitudes." In the report he proposed a seemingly wild idea, which was to build rockets that could travel to the moon. Thanks in large part to Goddard's research, the dream of journeying to the moon and beyond became a reality in the 20th century.

Goddard poses with one of his liquid fuel rockets at his lab in Roswell, New Mexico, in the 1930s.

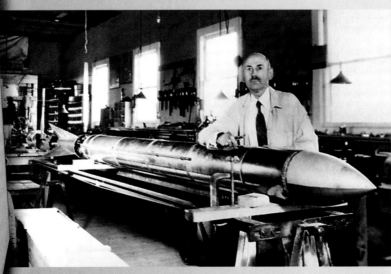

PRESSURE
RELIEF
VENT

LIQUID
OXYGEN
TANK

CORK
FLOAT
VALVES

OXYGEN GAS
PRESSURE LINE

CHECK
VALVE

Working out of a small laboratory in his hometown of Worcester, Massachusetts, Goddard used solid fuels such as gunpowder to power his early rockets. But solid fuels are hard to work with. It is very difficult to control the speed at which solid fuels burn or to stop the burning before they are used up. Goddard learned that for a rocket to successfully reach a specific height above Earth, the rocket needed to burn fuel at a controlled rate, just a little at a time. It also had to be possible to control when the fuel burned.

Goddard believed liquid fuel was the answer. He designed a rocket engine in which liquid fuel was pumped at a controllable rate into a combustion chamber, which is the enclosed space inside an engine where the fuel is burned. On March 16, 1926, Goddard launched the first successful liquid-fuel rocket from his Aunt Effie's farm.

The public didn't take Goddard's work seriously, however. Newspaper reporters wrote articles that made fun of his ideas about rocket flights to the moon. They even nicknamed him "Moony." Goddard responded by saying, "Every vision is a joke until the first man accomplishes it."

In 1930, Goddard was awarded a grant, which is money donated by an organization for a specific purpose. The grant made it possible for him to move his rocket research to Roswell, New Mexico. There Goddard continued to develop rockets for the rest of his life. He invented devices to keep a rocket on course so it would travel straight without wobbling. He experimented with multi-stage rockets, too. A multi-stage rocket has two or more engines that burn in sequence to boost the rocket higher and higher. One of Goddard's rockets reached an altitude of about 2.4 kilometers (1.5 miles). Another traveled so fast it exceeded the speed of sound.

Goddard at his Aunt Effie's farm in Auburn, Massachusetts

4

Goddard tows a rocket to its launch tower in New Mexico.

Goddard watches the launch of a rocket from a safe distance. New Mexico's clear skies made it a good place for testing rockets.

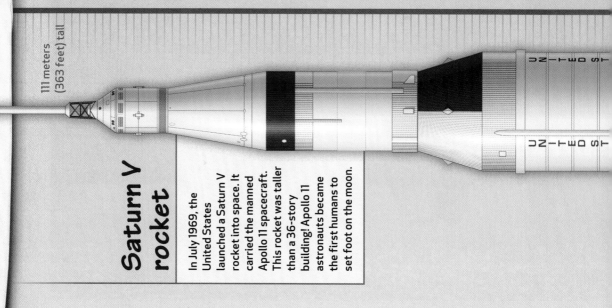

111 meters
(363 feet) tall

Saturn V rocket

In July 1969, the United States launched a Saturn V rocket into space. It carried the manned Apollo 11 spacecraft. This rocket was taller than a 36-story building! Apollo 11 astronauts became the first humans to set foot on the moon.

EVOLUTION OF THE ROCKET

By the time of his death in 1945, Goddard had launched more than 30 rockets of various designs. None of Goddard's own rockets ever made it into space. But his innovative research inspired the next generation of rocket scientists and laid the foundation for modern space exploration. Thanks to Goddard's persistence and creativity, scientists developed a series of rockets that helped transport humans to the moon and send **space probes** to distant planets. Goddard is so important to space exploration that the National Aeronautics and Space Administration (NASA) named the Goddard Space Flight Center in honor of the rocket pioneer. The flight center is located in Greenbelt, Maryland.

Molniya SL-6/A-2-e rocket

In January 1966, this rocket carried the Soviet moon probe *Luna 9* into space. *Luna 9* landed on the moon. It was a huge success. The pressure was on to see which country, the Soviet Union or the United States, would be first to land a human on the moon.

40 meters (131 feet) tall

Juno-1 rocket

On January 31, 1958, the United States sent its first satellite, *Explorer-I*, into orbit using a Juno-1 rocket.

21 meters (68 feet) tall

R-7 rocket

On October 4, 1957, the Soviet Union shocked the world by launching *Sputnik*, the first Earth-orbiting satellite. (The Soviet Union contained Russia and some neighboring countries.) The rocket that carried *Sputnik* into space was called the R-7. The launch of *Sputnik* started a "space race" between the United States and the Soviet Union.

29 meters (98 feet) tall

German V-2 rocket

During the 1930s, Goddard shared some of his research with German scientists. He stopped sharing before the start of World War II. He worried Germany might use rockets as weapons. That's exactly what happened. German V-2 rockets were based on Goddard's liquid-fuel designs.

13.5 meters (44 feet) tall

On March 16, 1926, Goddard made history by launching the world's first liquid fuel rocket. The rocket flew for just 2.5 seconds and traveled 12.5 meters (41 feet) into the air.

3.4 meters (11 feet) tall

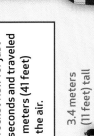
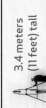

What do you think was Goddard's greatest contribution to rocket science?

Check In

GENRE Third-Person Narrative

Read to find out what it was like to walk on the moon.

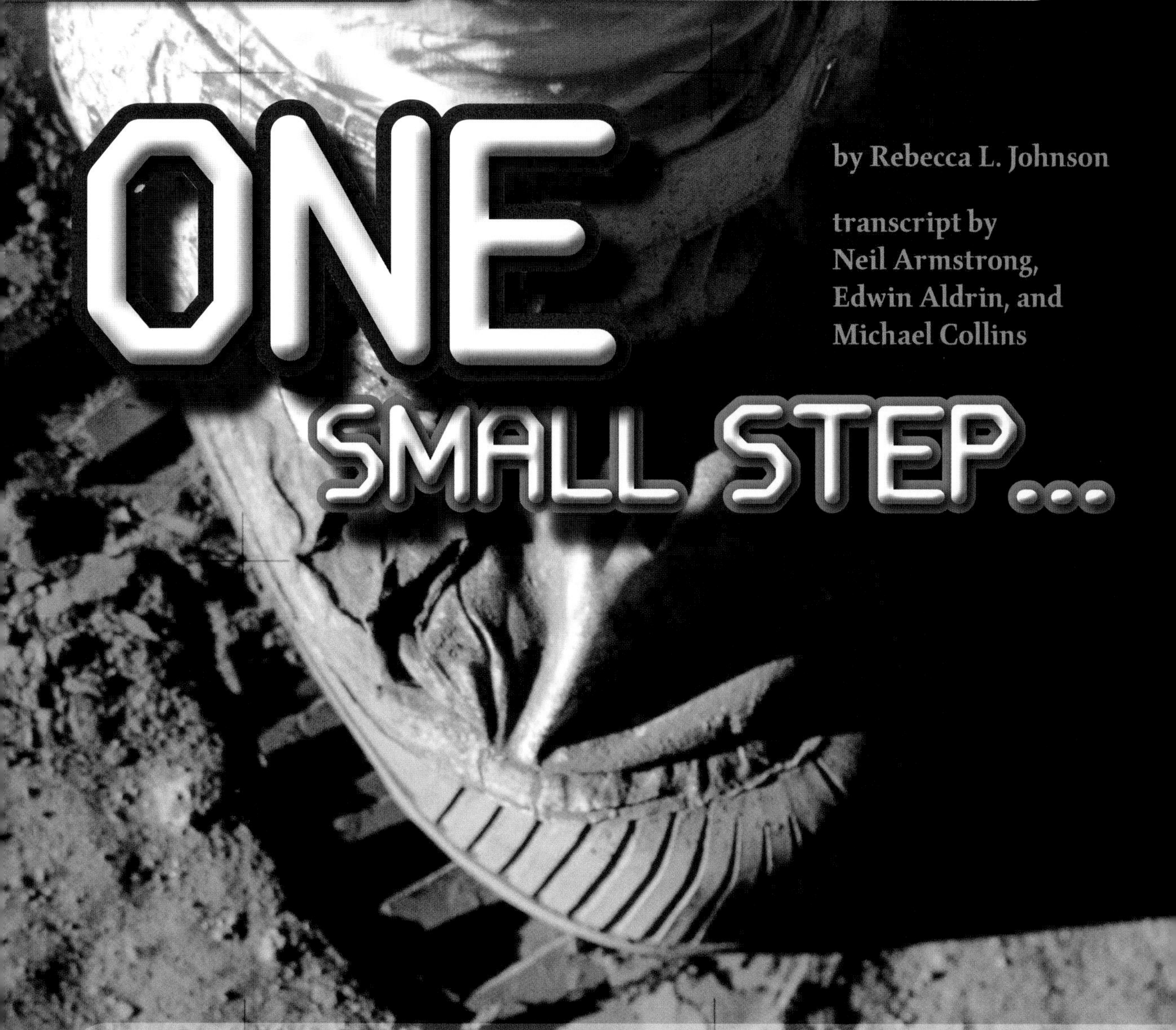

ONE SMALL STEP...

by Rebecca L. Johnson

transcript by Neil Armstrong, Edwin Aldrin, and Michael Collins

Live from the moon

On July 20, 1969, millions of people around the world saw those four words flash across their television screens. Then they watched, spellbound, as two American astronauts did what no one had ever done before. Wearing bulky spacesuits and backpacks of air to breathe, Neil Armstrong and Edwin "Buzz" Aldrin became the first human beings to walk on the moon.

How would you feel heading out into space, a rocket's engines roaring beneath you, facing the real possibility that you might never return? What would it be like to visit a place no one had ever seen firsthand? Can you imagine leaving the first footprints on Earth's closest

Neil Armstrong (1930–2012) was the commander of the Apollo 11 mission. He was the first person to walk on the moon.

Michael Collins served as command module pilot on the mission. He remained in orbit around the moon while Armstrong and Aldrin went to the moon's surface.

Edwin "Buzz" Aldrin was the lunar module pilot on the mission.

APOLLO 11

neighbor or looking out into space and seeing your home planet?

After centuries of people wondering what it would be like to travel to the moon, Armstrong, Aldrin, and astronaut Michael Collins successfully made the trip from Earth to the moon on board the Apollo 11 spacecraft. While Collins stayed with the **command module** in orbit around the moon, Armstrong and Aldrin descended to the moon's surface in a landing craft called the **lunar module.** From the moment the lunar module touched down, Armstrong and Aldrin were excited and in awe of where they were, and what their accomplishment meant for space exploration. Read on to share their experience—in their own words!

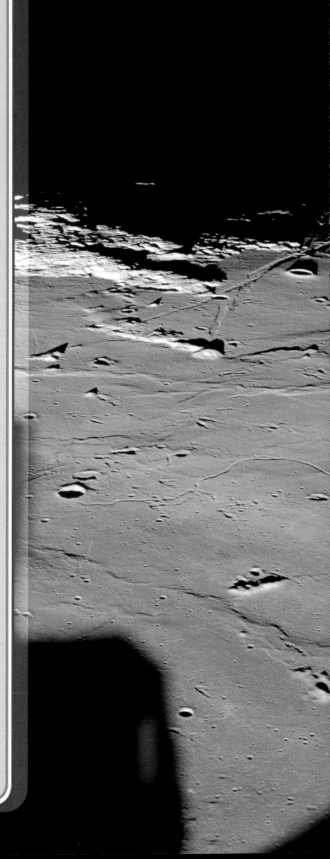

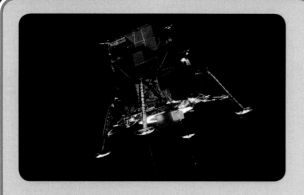

Touchdown

It is now 102 hours, 45 minutes, and 43 seconds after Apollo 11 launched into space. The lunar module, called Eagle, makes a risky landing in a shallow crater named the Sea of Tranquility. (Unknown to almost everyone back on Earth, Eagle has only 20 seconds of landing fuel to spare!) Armstrong and Aldrin keep up a running conversation with their Earth-based support team at the Johnson Space Center in Houston, Texas. CAPCOM is the nickname for the capsule communicator in Houston. Orbiting high overhead, astronaut Collins continues to pilot the command module called Columbia.

ARMSTRONG: Houston, [this is] Tranquility Base here. The Eagle has landed.

CAPCOM: Roger, Tranquility, we copy you on the ground. You got a bunch of guys about to turn blue. We're breathing again.

COLLINS (from *Columbia*): Fantastic!

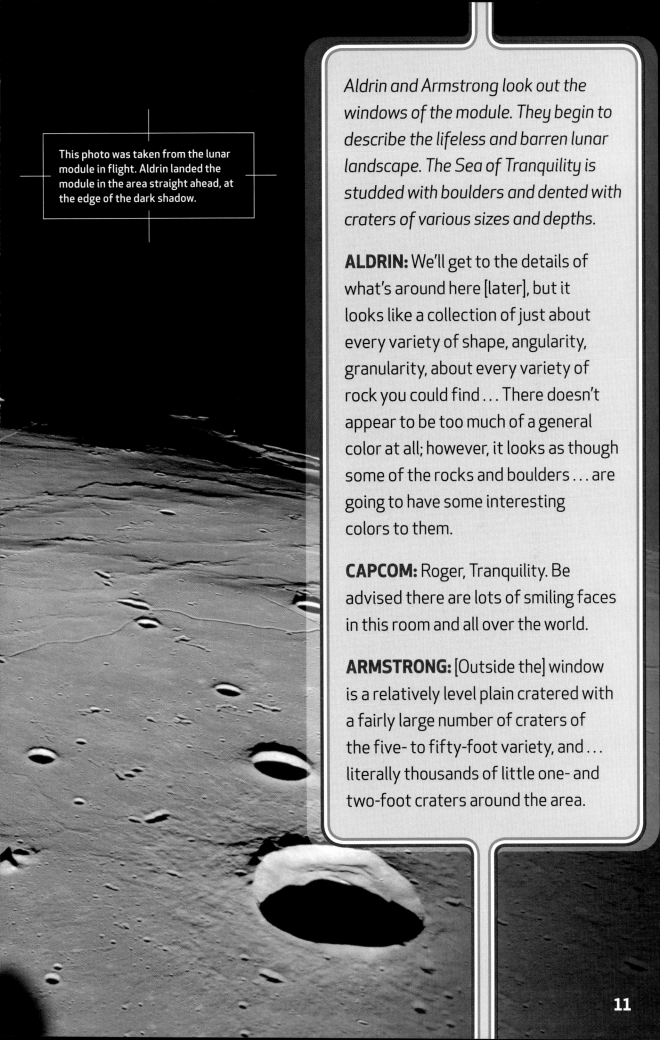

This photo was taken from the lunar module in flight. Aldrin landed the module in the area straight ahead, at the edge of the dark shadow.

Aldrin and Armstrong look out the windows of the module. They begin to describe the lifeless and barren lunar landscape. The Sea of Tranquility is studded with boulders and dented with craters of various sizes and depths.

ALDRIN: We'll get to the details of what's around here [later], but it looks like a collection of just about every variety of shape, angularity, granularity, about every variety of rock you could find ... There doesn't appear to be too much of a general color at all; however, it looks as though some of the rocks and boulders ... are going to have some interesting colors to them.

CAPCOM: Roger, Tranquility. Be advised there are lots of smiling faces in this room and all over the world.

ARMSTRONG: [Outside the] window is a relatively level plain cratered with a fairly large number of craters of the five- to fifty-foot variety, and ... literally thousands of little one- and two-foot craters around the area.

The two astronauts spend the next six-and-a-half hours making sure all the systems on the lunar module are working perfectly. After getting the go-ahead from Houston, Armstrong and Aldrin prepare to leave the lunar module. As mission commander, Armstrong is the first one out.

ARMSTRONG: The hatch is coming open ... OK, Houston, I'm on the porch.

CAPCOM: We're getting a picture on the TV ... OK, Neil, we can see you coming down the ladder now.

ARMSTRONG: I'm going to step off the LM [lunar module] now. That's one small step for [a] man, one giant leap for mankind. The surface is fine and powdery. I can ... kick it up loosely with my toe. It does adhere in fine layers like powdered charcoal to ... my boots. I only go in a small fraction of an inch, maybe an eighth of an inch, but I can see the footprints of my boots and the treads in the fine, sandy particles.

CAPCOM: Neil, this is Houston. We're copying.

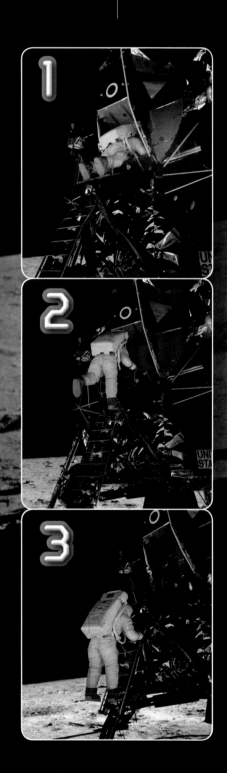

Armstrong snapped these photos as Aldrin left the lunar module.

ARMSTRONG: There seems to be no difficulty in moving around. As we suspected, it's even perhaps easier than the simulations … that we performed … on the ground.

One of Armstrong's first tasks is to collect a small sample of moon rocks and dust. Armstrong pauses to describe what he sees. It's hard for him to believe that he is truly standing on the moon.

ARMSTRONG: It has a stark beauty all its own. It's like much of the high desert of the United States. It's different but it's very pretty out here.

Twenty minutes later, astronaut Aldrin descends the ladder and joins Armstrong on the surface.

ALDRIN: Beautiful view!

ARMSTRONG: Isn't that something! Magnificent sight out here … Isn't it fun?

ALDRIN: The rocks are rather slippery … Hey, Neil, didn't I say we might see some purple rocks?

ARMSTRONG: Find a purple rock?

ALDRIN: Very small, sparkly fragments.

Knowing that millions of people on Earth are watching and listening, Armstrong describes and reads a plaque they brought to honor the historic landing. It states that the astronauts "came in peace for all mankind." The plaque will remain behind on the moon. Then the two men plant an American flag. Following a call from President Nixon, Armstrong and Aldrin set up several scientific experiments and continue collecting rock and soil samples.

ARMSTRONG: These boulders look like basalt [volcanic rock] and they have probably two percent white minerals in them.

ALDRIN (collecting a core sample): I hope you're watching how hard I have to hit this into the ground to the tune of about five inches, Houston.

ARMSTRONG: I'm picking up several pieces of really vesicular [pitted with small holes] rock out here now.

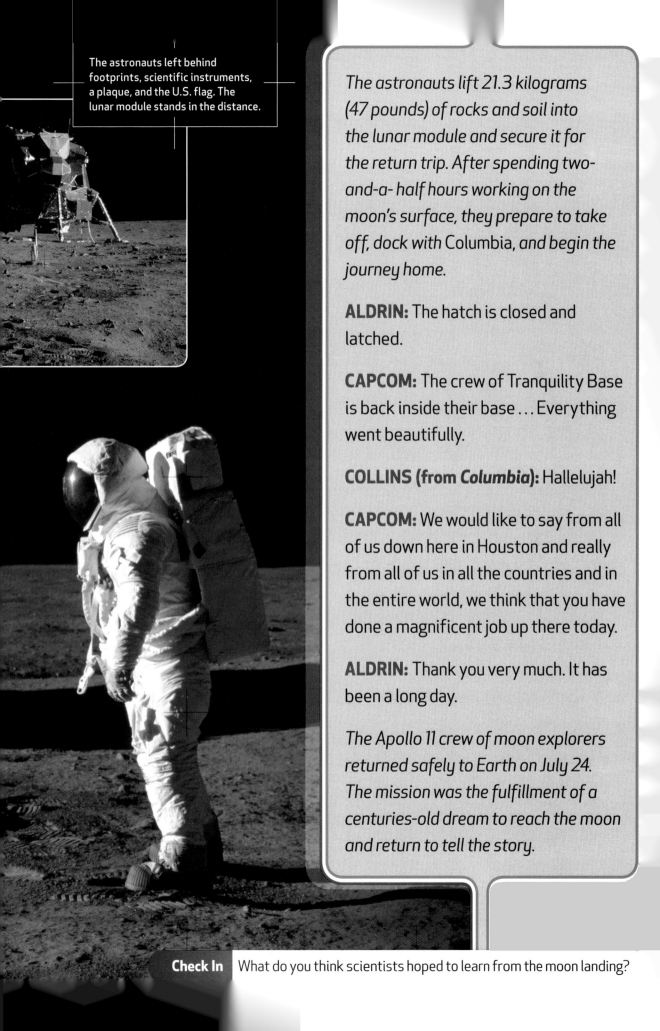

The astronauts left behind footprints, scientific instruments, a plaque, and the U.S. flag. The lunar module stands in the distance.

The astronauts lift 21.3 kilograms (47 pounds) of rocks and soil into the lunar module and secure it for the return trip. After spending two-and-a- half hours working on the moon's surface, they prepare to take off, dock with Columbia, and begin the journey home.

ALDRIN: The hatch is closed and latched.

CAPCOM: The crew of Tranquility Base is back inside their base . . . Everything went beautifully.

COLLINS (from *Columbia*): Hallelujah!

CAPCOM: We would like to say from all of us down here in Houston and really from all of us in all the countries and in the entire world, we think that you have done a magnificent job up there today.

ALDRIN: Thank you very much. It has been a long day.

The Apollo 11 crew of moon explorers returned safely to Earth on July 24. The mission was the fulfillment of a centuries-old dream to reach the moon and return to tell the story.

Check In What do you think scientists hoped to learn from the moon landing?

Far-Out MOO

by Rebecca L. Johnson

The word "moon" can refer to any rocky object that orbits a planet. Earth's moon is just one of dozens of moons in our **solar system.** The current count is more than 170. No doubt other moons are still waiting to be discovered.

Using **space probes** such as Voyagers 1 and 2, Galileo, Cassini, and the Hubble Space Telescope, scientists are able to explore the planets and their moons by photographing and mapping them. Such instruments are a scientist's eyes in space, sending back vast amounts of data and detailed pictures of some of the strangest places in our solar system and beyond.

Neptune

The planet Neptune is a cold gas giant 30 times farther from the sun than Earth. Neptune has 13 known moons, the largest of which is Triton. Triton was discovered in 1846 by an astronomer in England just 17 days after someone else discovered Neptune. Little is known about Neptune's smaller moons, but thanks to Voyager 2, scientists know quite a bit about Triton.

Triton To say Triton is cold doesn't do it justice. This moon is one of the coldest objects in the solar system. Its average temperature is about −235°C (−391°F). You'd think nothing much would be happening in such an extreme deep freeze. Triton, however, is surprisingly active. It's a world of "ice volcanoes."

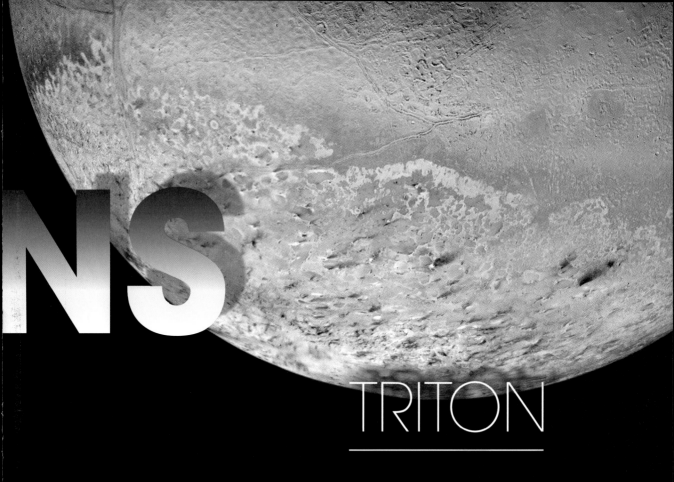

TRITON

These strange volcanoes spew out gases so cold they're in liquid form. The erupting liquids form droplets that instantly freeze and then drift back down to Triton's surface like snow. Voyager 2 snapped a picture of one erupting volcano ejecting a frigid, liquid cloud 8 kilometers (5 miles) out from Triton's surface.

Scientists think that, like Pluto, Triton may once have been a dwarf planet circling the sun in an orbit of its own. Then at some point, Triton was captured by the pull of Neptune's gravity.

Triton is doomed. Neptune's gravity is gradually drawing Triton closer and closer. Millions of years from now, Triton will

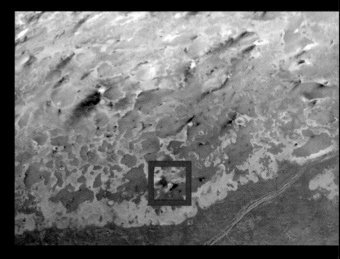

∧ Dark streaks reveal some 50 "ice volcanoes" near Triton's south pole. Some are more than 161 kilometers (100 miles) long. The red box contains at least three ice volcanoes.

edge so close to Neptune that the planet's powerful gravitational pull will tear Triton apart. Scientists think the remaining debris might form a ring around Neptune, like a memorial to what Triton once was.

Saturn

Saturn is second only to Jupiter in the number of moons it possesses—62 known moons in all. Scientists are particularly interested in two of Saturn's largest moons: the oversized snowball Enceladus and gigantic, mysterious Titan.

Enceladus Enceladus is the whitest, brightest object in the solar system, thanks to a surface that is thick with ice and snow. This moon is so bright because it reflects almost all of the sunlight that strikes it.

Yet as hard and frozen as Enceladus seems to be, there are geysers on its surface, mostly near the moon's south pole. A geyser is like a volcano that spews out water instead of lava. Enormous jets of water vapor and ice crystals erupt from Enceladus's geysers.

ENCELADUS

∨ Jets of ice and water vapor shoot from Enceladus's geysers. The Cassini space probe took this image from a distance of about 148,000 kilometers (92,000 miles).

TITAN

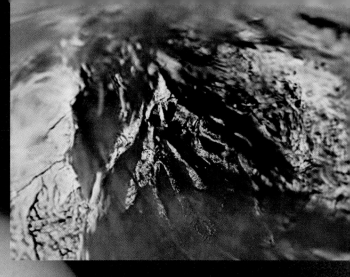

∧ The Huygens probe captured this image of mountains and valleys on Titan.

Titan It's taken scientists a long time to learn about Titan, Saturn's largest moon. That's because its dense atmosphere blocked any clear view of the surface until early 2005, when scientists got their first look at what Titan is really like. A small probe named Huygens detached from Cassini and dove down through Titan's murky atmosphere, taking pictures along the way.

The pictures show a world that resembles a super-cold version of ancient Earth. Titan has mountains and valleys, wind-sculpted dunes, and flat plains. It also has shimmering lakes, branching rivers, and rain clouds. But it isn't water that fills these lakes, rivers, and clouds. Any water on Titan is frozen solid because the temperature there is about −178°C (−289°F). The rains, rivers, and lakes are liquid methane and other substances that would be in a gaseous state in a warmer place such as Earth.

Jupiter

Jupiter has the most known moons of any planet in the solar system—an astounding 66! Jupiter's four biggest moons are Ganymede, Io, Europa, and Callisto. They were first spotted through a telescope by the Italian astronomer Galileo Galilei in the 17th century. Io and Europa especially interest scientists today.

Io The third-largest of Jupiter's moons, Io is the fiery nightmare of the solar system. Shaken by constant eruptions and explosions, it's the most volcanically active place scientists have ever seen. Lava flows out of giant cracks and streams into huge lava lakes. Enormous clouds of gas shoot up from massive volcanoes. The clouds contain sulfur, which drifts back down to the surface like golden snow, giving this volcanic moon its yellow color. Yet away from the lava lakes and volcanoes, temperatures on Io plunge to –150°C (–238°F).

The Voyager 1 space probe discovered Io's volcanoes in 1979. The Galileo space probe has since been there, too. A recent review of data suggests that Io has a vast sea of melted rock lurking beneath its surface.

∨ Io's many freckles are huge volcanoes. Eruptions are so frequent that Io's surface is continually changing.

IO

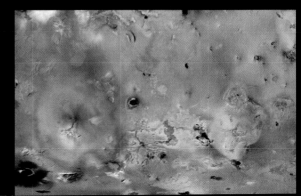

EUROPA

The brown areas show where rocky material has mixed into Europa's icy crust. The lines are huge cracks. Some cracks are more than 3,000 kilometers (1,850 miles) long.

Europa Europa couldn't be more different from Io. Jupiter's fourth-largest moon is an icy world, covered in a frozen crust of water ice that is riddled with ridges and cracks. Scientists believe, however, that beneath Europa's frozen surface lies a warmer heart: a deep global ocean of salty liquid water. If life exists beyond Earth, Europa's hidden ocean might be a good place to look.

The space probe Galileo made several flybys of Europa. Galileo provided scientists with clues about Europa's covered ocean and spectacular images of its frozen surface. Voyager 1, Voyager 2, and Cassini have also captured pictures of this chilly moon.

Check In How do space probes help scientists in ways that Earth-based telescopes cannot?

STORMS IN SPACE

by Rebecca L. Johnson

On the weekend of July 15, 2012, the night sky above Cotton, Minnesota, looked like it was on fire. Bands of red, orange, and green light rippled above the horizon. Sky watchers gazed up at the beautiful light show, which lasted for more than 36 hours but was visible only at night. These sky lights, called **auroras,** flared and flashed in the Southern Hemisphere, too. What caused the light show? Explosive activity on our star, the sun.

"Auroras are the visible sign of a solar storm arriving from space, a storm set in motion by changes on the sun," says Dr. Madhulika Guhathakurta, also known as Dr. G. She is the head of NASA's Living With a Star program, which works to understand changes in the sun and how those changes affect **space weather.** Space weather is the changing conditions in space that can

DR. MADHULIKA GUHATHAKURTA is a NASA scientist. She has spent much of her scientific career studying the sun. In addition to her work with the Living With a Star program, she is part of an international research effort involving all the world's space agencies to try to better understand space weather.

affect our planet and our technology, including satellites, radio, and even our electricity supply.

The sun is the driving force behind space weather. The sun's extreme heat produces tiny, superhot particles. These particles shoot out into space. Scientists call this constant stream of particles

peacefully, like a gentle breeze. But violent eruptions on the sun's surface can produce solar storms—powerful "gusts" of solar wind that stream through space.

When solar storms slam into Earth's atmosphere, they can produce bursts of light energy: the auroras that swirl and

SPACE WEATHER

"We know quite a lot about the sun," explains Dr. G. "The sun is the biggest, most massive object in the **solar system.** It holds the planets in orbit. It heats Earth and makes it livable. It warms my skin on summer days, turns the sky blue, and lights up the beautiful world around me."

Scientists are learning more about how the sun produces space weather. This weather is not like the weather on Earth. It consists of huge bursts of energy that erupt from the surface of the sun and whiz through space.

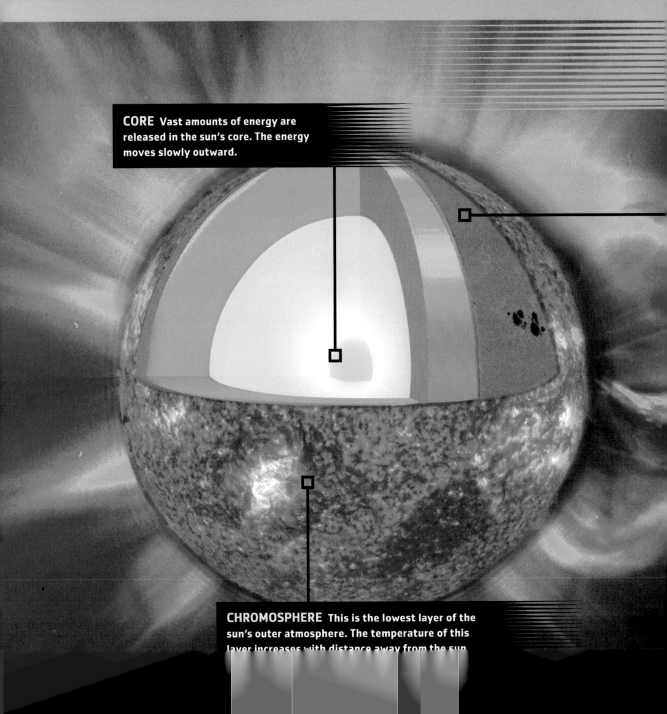

CORE Vast amounts of energy are released in the sun's core. The energy moves slowly outward.

CHROMOSPHERE This is the lowest layer of the sun's outer atmosphere. The temperature of this layer increases with distance away from the sun.

The sun is a gigantic sphere of superheated, gas-like matter called plasma. "The plasma is converted into energy in the sun's core," explains Dr. G. "The energy moves from the core to the outer layers of the sun, and then is released into the solar system. The sun generates incredible amounts of energy. In one second, the sun produces enough energy to meet the world's energy demands for the next million years!"

Driven by this energy engine, the sun's gas-like plasma is constantly on the move. It churns, pops, and explodes at the sun's surface. Sometimes the plasma erupts violently. These eruptions happen near sunspots, which are darker, slightly cooler patches on the sun's outer surface. Eruptions send billions of tons of particles hurtling into space. What happens when Earth is in the path of one of these storms?

PHOTOSPHERE This is the sun's visible boundary. Close up, it has a grainy texture caused by the bubbling of super-hot particles.

CORONA The halo-like corona is the outermost layer of the sun's atmosphere. The corona is the source of solar wind and solar eruptions.

EARTH'S MAGNETIC FIELD The magnetic field that surrounds Earth acts like a shield. It deflects most solar wind away from the planet. But severe solar storms can push far enough into the field to cause trouble.

STORM DAMAGE

"Auroras are beautiful, not dangerous or destructive," explains Dr. G. "However, they can be a sign of trouble. Auroras tell us of the presence of solar storms. Most solar storms are harmless, but big storms can cause problems."

Solar storms can interfere with the sending and receiving of radio waves. "The most common kind of problem is a radio blackout—a temporary loss of radio communication," says Dr. G.

"Sometimes, airline flights have to change course to avoid flying over the Arctic Circle where radio blackouts are most common." Solar storms can also affect electronics by silencing cell phones and communications satellites.

In addition, severe solar storms generate powerful electric currents that can travel down to Earth's surface and shut down electric power grids. Storm-zapped

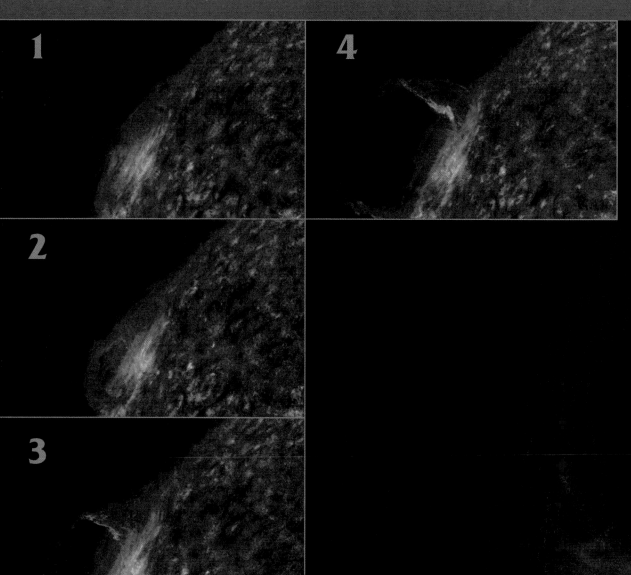

1

4

2

3

power grids don't just leave people in the dark, either.

"A really big solar storm could break your toilet," says Dr. G. "How? By making it impossible to flush. In many cities, the water supply relies on electric pumps. If the power goes out, as can happen during a big solar storm, the pumps will stop pumping, so the water will stop flowing. Then there will be no water for bathrooms! By knocking out power, solar storms can put a stop to anything that requires electricity—from toilets to television."

The world has become increasingly dependent on technology that needs electricity to work, so people are at greater risk from destructive solar storms. That's why it's important to keep a close watch on the sun.

5

Size of Earth ➞

An eruption on the sun's surface sends out a stream of energy. What if Earth was in the path of this energy stream? It could result in auroras. It could also result in widespread blackouts.

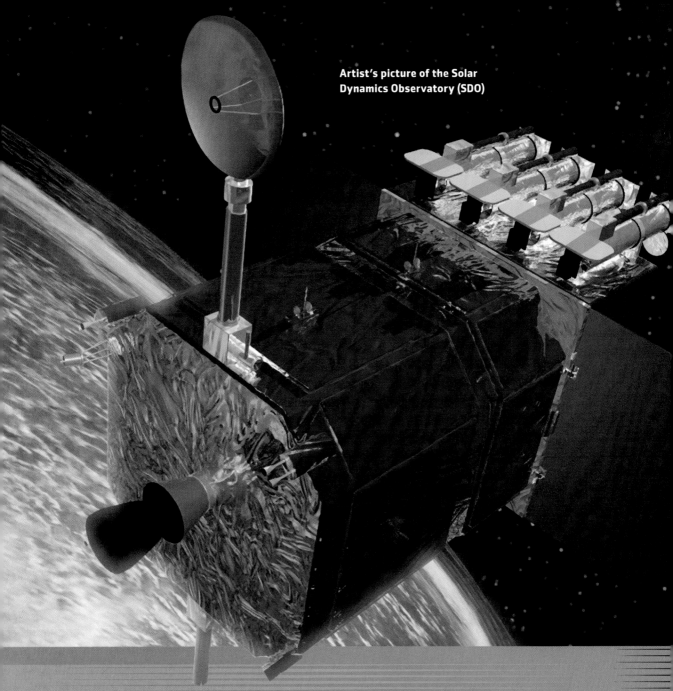

Artist's picture of the Solar
Dynamics Observatory (SDO)

CLOSE-UP ON THE SUN

Weather forecasters gather information about wind, temperature, and air pressure to help them predict the weather on Earth. Dr. G and her team at NASA monitor the sun, space, and solar winds to better predict space weather. Their most important monitoring tools are **space probes.**

Launched in 2010, the Solar Dynamics Observatory (SDO) was the first probe to head into space under the Living With a Star program. SDO gathers data about the sun's surface and interior.

The "eyes" that SDO keeps on the sun are particularly sharp ones, too. Its instruments take pictures that have ten

Dr. G and other solar scientists review data from SDO.

Scientists use light of different wavelengths to study the sun. For example, this wavelength provides good views of the sun's corona.

times better resolution than a high-definition TV. These pictures of the sun are big and crisp enough to fill the screen of an IMAX theater. And the space probe snaps one picture every 10 seconds! The amount of information SDO beams to Earth every 24 hours is enormous, roughly the same as downloading half a million songs, or 380 full-length movies.

Dr. G is rightfully proud of SDO and the views of the sun it provides. According to Dr. G, SDO "promises to transform solar physics in the same way the Hubble Space Telescope has transformed astronomy."

SEEING DOUBLE

The Solar Terrestrial Relations Observatory (STEREO) is another tool helping scientists track changes on the sun that can lead to solar storms. STEREO is actually two nearly identical space probes that work together.

Both STEREO probes circle the sun in almost the same orbit as Earth. One probe travels a little faster than Earth, while the second probe travels a little slower. As a result, the two probes view the sun from different angles. When the pictures they take are combined, the result is a 3-dimensional view of the sun.

Since they were launched, the two STEREO probes have been slowly moving farther apart from each other in their orbits. In February 2011, the probes reached the point where they were on opposite sides of the sun. This made it possible for them to view all of the far

An artist's picture of the two STEREO spacecraft in orbit around the sun

side of the sun, giving scientists a 360-degree view of our star for the first time.

"Observatories such as SDO and STEREO are very important for space weather forecasting," says Dr. G. "These observatories can see all sides of the sun—the near side and the far side. Nothing escapes their attention. When a solar storm leaves the sun and heads for Earth, the spacecraft can track it, which helps forecasters predict when it will reach our planet."

Thanks to SDO, STEREO, and other solar observatories, scientists can more accurately predict when a solar storm will strike Earth. Scientists can also predict how bad the storm might be. That's very good news, especially now. After years of relative quiet, the sun is entering a more active phase. There might be stormy space weather ahead!

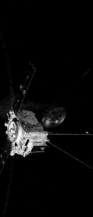

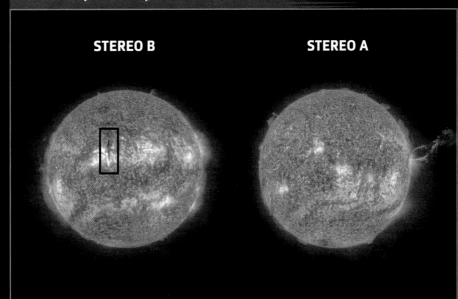

Each probe photographs the sun at the same time, but from a different angle. Look carefully at the photo from STEREO B. Do you see the dark vertical line inside the black box? That's the solar eruption in the photo from STEREO A.

STEREO B   STEREO A

Check In How might severe space weather affect you?

Discuss

1. What do you think connects the four pieces in *Exploring Above and Beyond*? What makes you think that?

2. Explain why Robert Goddard is often considered the father of modern rocket technology. Use examples in your answer.

3. Compare and contrast the astronauts' descriptions of Earth's moon in "One Small Step . . ." to one of the moons in "Far-Out Moons." Explain how a landing on that far-out moon might be different from the Apollo 11 landing on Earth's moon.

4. Explain how storms on the sun produce space weather. How can space weather affect Earth?

5. What questions do you still have about the sun, Earth's moon, or other moons in the solar system? How might you go about finding more information?